TOM HANKS

TOM HANKS

GRETA ROSE

CONTENTS

CHAPTER 1

Disclaimer

The content in this book is intended for informational and entertainment purposes only. While every effort has been made to ensure the accuracy of the information presented, the author and publisher make no representations or warranties of any kind, express or implied, about the completeness, accuracy, reliability, suitability, or availability with respect to the content of this book.

The views and opinions expressed in this book are those of the author and do not necessarily reflect the official policy or position of any individual, company, or organization mentioned. Any resemblance to actual persons, living or dead, or actual events is purely coincidental.

This book is not intended to defame, libel, or slander any person, company, or organization. All references to individuals, companies, products, and brands are for illustrative purposes only, and no affiliation with or endorsement by them is intended or implied.

The author and publisher disclaim any responsibility for any actions or outcomes resulting from the application of information contained in this book. Readers should seek professional advice or conduct their own research when making decisions based on the content provided.

CHAPTER 2

Introduction

Tom Hanks does not simply play a decent person onscreen. In many ways, he is a respected symbol of credibility and kindness in an otherwise appearance-driven industry. Besides state governors, religious figures, and future presidential candidates, who peaks Presidential approval ratings? The correct answer may surprise you. Tom Hanks. Critics, on the other hand, adored Studio Ghibli and French films with impenetrable subtitles. So, this list is about the opposite of that. Tom Hanks was also a likeable leading actor for most of his career. He was Burns, and we were all Marge.

His big-screen work, such as Steven Spielberg and Robert Zemeckis, sometimes undermined his reputation, but most of his work, especially the roles that garnered him Oscar nominations for Big, Philadelphia, Forrest Gump, Saving Private Ryan, and Cast Away, practically made him America's reassuring brother. While there are several avenues to pursue when considering Tom Hanks and his contribution to the industry, in the following piece, we would argue that his evolution from television comedic bit player to cinema industry giant has had a lasting effect. In this article, we will take a closer look at Hanks' earlier television performances, examine the impact of his second feature film, and discuss his enshrinement as "America's Favorite Actor" in the 21st century.

CHAPTER 3

Early Life and Career

Thomas J. Hanks, known as Tom Hanks, was born on July 9, 1956. Hanks grew up in California, and his father had many jobs, including working with the school district. His parents divorced, and his father started a restaurant, which he ran after marrying Tom's stepmother, Frances Wong, who is of Chinese descent. Hanks has three siblings: two brothers and a sister. His older brother, Jim, also became an actor and filmmaker. In college, Hanks found that he enjoyed acting. He transferred to California State University in Sacramento and attended school, worked at a pizza parlor, and found non-academic theater work to keep busy.

Hanks got his professional start at the Great Lakes Shakespeare Festival in Cleveland, where he performed for three years. He met and married Samantha Lewes and had two children. After Hanks and Lewes divorced, Hanks married Rita Wilson, with whom he had two sons. After the festival, he went to New York. In 1980, he played a number of bit parts in films and on television. For three years, he played Kip Wilson on the ABC television series Bosom Buddies. Hanks got his break in movies in 1984 when he appeared as the leading character in Splash. The film did very well; in 1985, he was cast as the leading character in the romantic comedy The Man with One Red Shoe. He also made three movies in 1986. In 1994, Hanks won an Academy Award and a Golden Globe for his performance in Philadelphia. The next year, he got his second Oscar and a Golden Globe for his role in Forrest Gump. He has won numerous other awards as well, and he is well-known for his performances in such films as Saving Private Ryan, Cast Away, The Terminal, Cars, Charlie Wilson's War, and Larry Crowne.

CHAPTER 4

Breakthrough Films

The 'Breakthrough Films' section delves into the milestone movies and projects that marked a turning point in Tom Hanks' career. It provides an analysis of the films that propelled him to fame and established his reputation as a versatile and talented actor, contributing to his enduring popularity.

Breakthrough Films

Before Tom Hanks embarked on these multiple projects, his career advanced incrementally - major project by major project. The most significant among those early movies, the project that made him a marquee name, was Big, about an adolescent boy who awakens one morning to find that he is the adult Tom Hanks. The complexity of making that fanciful storyline credible fell squarely on the slender shoulders of Hanks, and the miracle was that he accomplished it. "Essentially," Jack Garner wrote in Gannett Newspapers, "the story's humor comes out of the interaction of two people who are the same person at different stages of growth." The plot is childishly bright and playful, and Hanks, playfully and brightly, ratchets up the performance to an appropriate level, expressing emotions that are part boy and part man (when he's not showing off in a toy store). "This role," Kendrick wrote in Futurist, "has become the film that people remember Hanks for." Horton summed it up by calling Big Tom Hanks' "first truly bankable project."

Even more notable, though, was another film of 1988, Punchline, which showed once again the range that Hanks as an actor possessed. The film is about people who are deeply into something, and there is a sense of inherent logic in casting an academy-award winning actor who once studied to be a writer to play the part of a stand-up comic. Garner's distinction in Gannett Newspapers was unequivocal: "Punchline gives Hanks a chance to do the kind of full-tilt, dramatic role that made him famous." The movie sank without a trace at the box office, but it has only burnished Hanks' acting status as it has receded. When Push and Big Come to Shove remarked that Punchline gave him a chance to display his dramatic talent, as well as collaborate with a tight ensemble, and is effectively dazzling." Tom Hanks wasn't merely a popular teenager; he was his generation's charismatic host. He was also its favorite actor, and that bonus has steadily blossomed into a fortuitous advantage for Hollywood's favorite leading man.

CHAPTER 5

Versatility in Acting

Throughout his career, Tom Hanks has portrayed assorted personas on the big screen. Primarily known for his work in iconic films like Forrest Gump, A League of Their Own, and Apollo 13, Hanks has also ventured into the comedy genre, especially during his early years as an actor. Some of his lighter films include Turner & Hooch (1989) and Joe Versus the Volcano (1990). His ability to master a persona of goofiness and vulnerability was conveyed onscreen, especially when paired with the expert comedy of both David S. Ward and Joe Dante. Not only has Hanks showcased a wide range in dramatic storytelling, he has also been able to move audiences with the endearing characters he has brought to life in timeless romantic favorites Sleepless in Seattle and You've Got Mail.

As an actor, Hanks has received acclaim for the diverse roles that he has played throughout the years. His portrayal of a man living with AIDS in the 1993 film Philadelphia won him his first Oscar for Best Actor. Similarly, his portrayal of an emotionally demanding role in Cast Away showed Hanks' ability to adroitly use his athleticism, stark expressions, and body movements. His performance of a man stranded on a deserted island won him a 2000 Golden Globe Award for Best Actor in a Motion Picture for Drama. After his roles in the aforementioned films, Hanks showcased an empathetic civil-

ity that most people can identify with. As Woody, children and animation fans alike were drawn to the toy cowboy character, regardless
of his naive optimism. Actor Matthew McConaughey once referred
to Hanks as "citizen of cinema," someone who brings morality and
emotional truths to every film that he is attached to. The gentle portrayal of the animation earned rounds of applause from audiences.

Hollywood Icon Status

For over 30 years, Tom Hanks has been a household name and a bankable actor. He is often referred to as "America's dad," a phrase that suggests his status as a popular and beloved figure. He was a star of a generation of actors that became iconic for the roles they played during the 80s and 90s, like Tom Cruise and Julia Roberts. While Cruise and Roberts are more likely to make news with drunken party photos or on-set outbursts, Hanks has cultivated a reputation as an everyman. He doesn't live in an ivory tower like some of his contemporaries might. His money does not distance him from the public. Hanks recognized and exploited trends and managed to stay a viable leading man in Hollywood for a very long time. All of these factors contribute to an overall attitude that Hanks is a genuine person and not, in fact, a character played by an actor on a screen. And it's not to argue with Hanks' portrayal as a caring father figure in that news.

This overall attitude of hobbyist stems from 69 box-office hits, 32 major award wins, and numerous nominations between 1984 and 2020. From "Splash" to "Greyhound," "Sleepless in Seattle" to all four "Toy Story" films. Hanks also became the fourth lead actor in history to win back-to-back Academy Awards with "Philadelphia" and "Forrest Gump" in 1993 and 1994, respectively. What could possibly sour his reputation in the eyes of the general public about the common good consensus? The fact that Hanks has been working at a high level for over 30 years and his eventual wider body of work ensures his place in popular culture.

CHAPTER 7

Impact on American Cinema

Related to impact on American cinema, exploiting his earliest beginning, Tom Hanks advanced his profession to become one of the best actors in American cinematic history. Through his use of raw talent and genuine determination, Hanks' reach made significant strides into shifting the way in which war films are produced, such as Saving Private Ryan. Not only this, but Hanks has helped to bring renewed excitement through his historic dramatizations. Recalling the likes of Apollo 13 and The Da Vinci Code, viewers gasped in awe at the spectacle that Hanks portrayed.

In recent years, Hanks has perpetuated his impact as one of our greatest actors by adopting the role of Disney character Woody. Appearing in four films of Toy Story, audiences were eagerly waiting five years after the third, and announced to be the final, installment to see their favorite characters back on the silver screen. Hanks has inserted a tremendous amount of personality into his self-named character. Vocally embellishing a love for caring for his child and further companions, Woody became a heartwarming extension to how we view sheriffs in the old American West. With a timeless impact, it is without a doubt that Hanks' legacy will carry on through the world of film. It can be said that Tom Hanks genuinely loves humankind. He demonstrated that in the roles he chose to play, in the directions he has chosen to exploit those roles, and in the respect he pays to those for whom the stories are inspired by. As one of America's most adored actors, Tom Hanks has been a recipient of several prestigious awards and has appeared in over three dozen films that exude class. In exploring his six most memorable roles, we can get an understanding of what makes Hanks "America's favorite actor".

CHAPTER 8

Awards and Recognition

Tom Hanks has won numerous awards throughout his career, including five People's Choice Awards, nine Emmy Award nominations, six Golden Globe Award nominations (with two wins), and two Oscars. He has also won an American Comedy Award, a Critics' Choice Movie Award, three Screen Actors Guild Awards, a Bafta Award, and an AFI Lifetime Achievement Award. More than a few diverse short notes on Tom Hanks have been penned over the years. Tom Hanks very well may be America's favorite actor—and his affable manner, solid performances, and box office and/or television sitcom ratings track record would seem to validate that status. Sometimes it seems that just about everybody in the whole wide world may just love Tom Hanks. Ask Joe World-diplomat about foreign relations and then about Tom Hanks' acting career.

During the years between 1995 and 2005, Tom Hanks won back-to-back Academy Awards for his performances in the movies Philadelphia (1993) and Forrest Gump (1994). As for Forrest Gump, Tom Hanks' portrayal of that character in that movie is the golden standard of Lake Wobegon performances. And then from 1998 on, in a gesture perhaps intended to put things right with the universe, Tom Hanks was nominated for several additional Academy Awards because no, actually, he really deserved it: three best actor nominations in the three years 1998-2000, for Saving Private Ryan (1998), "You've Got Mail" (1999), and "Cast Away".

CHAPTER 9

Philanthropy and Social Causes

Tom Hanks once stated in an interview that those who had ascended to his level of success had a responsibility to use that platform for good. He has typically led by example in the realm of philanthropy. Hanks and his wife, actress Rita Wilson, founded the Playtone Foundation, which seeks to highlight the impact of individual stories on the larger world. Hanks serves as a board member of the World Wildlife Fund and has been a long-time donor to environmental causes. Hanks has supported a staggering number of charities for years. This includes an initiative to build a mile-and-a-half long park in place of a freeway ravine in Seattle. He and his wife have donated large sums to the ACLU and V-Day, a charity organization that seeks to end violence against women. Hanks is also a philanthropist on a smaller, more community level. For example, he has donated to build a new inner city school, after learning that the only school in that area was riddled with drugs.

Hanks has become a spokesman for social advocacy as well. On May 24th, 2017, Hanks advocated for students to the crowd gathered on the Stanford University campus to hear the college commencement speech. "We are going to do all the self-centered things you'd expect from a bunch of 19 to 22-year-olds. And if you're not careful, you'll wake up at 40 and your whole life will be a version of Stanford Law Steve Mnuchin who will have no idea he was a movie producer on the first Iron Man movie, which he is," he said of Steven T. Mnuchin. "Don't vote for Steve Mnuchin, ladies and gentlemen. Do not let this embarrassment of a man be the president of the United States." His advocacy for worthy causes also extends into the humanitarian realm. In 2003 and 2004, Hanks spoke on NBC TV network, the Fox TV Network, and CNN in an effort to increase awareness of the globe's refugee crisis. He has lent his support to refugees of the decade-long conflicts in Sudan, including the war raging in the western region of the country. He has contributed to raising awareness of the needs of more than 2.5 million people who died in the region of Darfur, in the same country. For Hanks, fame provides the power to get his message across and "turn up the volume" when he's speaking out for refugees, an official explained in a 2006 interview.

CHAPTER 10

Personal Life and Family

Hanks was married to American actress Samantha Lewes in 1978, whom he met while attending college. The two shared two children together, a son who Hanks affectionately referred to as Truman Theodore and daughter, actress Elizabeth Hanks. Unfortunately, the couple's marriage ended in divorce in 1987. After his divorce from Lewes, Hanks married actress Rita Wilson in 1988. The couple met during the filming of the popular 1980's television show, Bosom Buddies. Just like his previous marriage, Hanks and Wilson welcomed two children into their life. Hanks also took on step-father responsibilities, helping to raise Wilson's two children from her previous marriage.

Hanks is also a doting grandparent to four children. Although all of his children have been involved in the entertainment industry, taking on careers in acting, writing, music, and voice acting, Hanks' children have largely steered clear of the glitz and glamour that society often associates with Hollywood. Instead, they are leading private lives, focusing on their careers and their own personal relationships. Hanks revealed in 2007 that he had contracted type 2 diabetes and taking an additional PR campaign in Japan while becoming the face of for the Japanese national Hitachi staple line as of 2016. He is a motivational speaker for a number he calls "Hanksisms," where he tries to pass on the large amounts of wisdom he has collected over the years to upcoming actors.

CHAPTER 11

Conclusion

The American public has been drawn to Tom Hanks, following his filmography from his break in Bosom Buddies to his recent roles in News of the World and A Man Called Ove. There has been a Tom Hanks film or promotional material about a Hanks movie at least once a year every year since 1980. Through humor and likability, Tom Hanks has shown that an actor can become more than an actor; through his films, Hanks has become a part of the audience's family.

Tom Hanks's hard work and likable screen presence has led him to become wildly popular amongst American households. His supporting roles line movies, Netflix, and TV screens. He is involved with television production, appearing as himself in documentaries, and promoting his many films and streaming productions. With an ability to appeal to all ages, ethnicities, and social classes, Hanks is a true family man. His unique ability to be professional on screen and off while letting his heart show in his performances makes Tom Hanks a wonderful choice for America's Favorite Actor. In the multitude of reasons given for being Hanks' best film, the idea that Tom Hanks is a modern-day everyman remains vital to the actor's on-screen persona; Hanks's appeal also reflects his ability to inhabit characters who share this relatability. Over time, audiences have watched Hanks himself grow and change. In his more recent roles, Hanks portrays a less naive "everyman" and takes on darker, more dramatic roles as a considerate and thought-provoking "everyman".